A Voice from the Valley

A Voice from the Valley

Tim Dustin

RESOURCE *Publications* • Eugene, Oregon

A VOICE FROM THE VALLEY

Copyright © 2021 Tim Dustin. All rights reserved. Except for brief quotations in critical publications or reviews, no part of this book may be reproduced in any manner without prior written permission from the publisher. Write: Permissions, Wipf and Stock Publishers, 199 W. 8th Ave., Suite 3, Eugene, OR 97401.

Resource Publications
An Imprint of Wipf and Stock Publishers
199 W. 8th Ave., Suite 3
Eugene, OR 97401

www.wipfandstock.com

PAPERBACK ISBN: 978-1-6667-0066-4
HARDCOVER ISBN: 978-1-6667-0067-1
EBOOK ISBN: 978-1-6667-0068-8

05/07/21

For you, God.
May my story be an acceptable offering.

Contents

Our Only Hope | 3
Who's Driving This Thing? | 4
Creeping Crickets | 5
Naked & Afraid | 6
I Know | 7
Run, Rabbit | 8
Brothers & Sisters | 8
Beggars & Kings | 9
That Broken Man Is Me | 10
Not Overcome | 12
Pain the Devil | 13
Babel | 14
You | 14
Darkness, My Old Friend | 16
Our God | 17
The Moment of Surrender | 18
Only Human | 19
Of Clay | 21
The "Can-Do" Attitude | 22
Mission Control | 23
To Find Peace & Rest | 24
Someone Tell Me Why | 26
Spitting Tar | 28
Dive, Dive | 30
Twenty Thousand Leagues Under | 31
Amazing Love | 34
Isaac on the Altar | 35
A-C-T-I-O-N | 37
They're Dimming the Lights Now | 38

Afterword | 41
Acknowledgements | 45

Before I was ever born,
God had his eye on this sparrow

—ERIC MCILVEEN

Our Only Hope

ONE OF MY WRITING professors once gave me the advice, "Just shut up and write the thing," and I think that's what I have to do, otherwise I'll never get started. It's hard to say what this is going to be about, because I'm really not too sure at this point. I'm praying God will guide me and guide my words and hopefully only the right ones will make it out onto these pages.

I graduated from undergrad with a 3.9 GPA and recently graduated grad school with a 4.0 GPA, and yet I can't find a job anywhere. I've been looking for six months now, have sent out dozens and dozens of applications, and there's been nothing, barely a response from any of them. I'm educated, right? Shouldn't any place be lucky to have me?

However, if only good things happened to "good" people and only bad things happened to bad people, life would be fair, almost perfect, but it doesn't take much these days to look around and see how broken it all is.

I've been diagnosed with generalized anxiety disorder, which has recently been a thorn in my side like I've never imagined in my darkest dreams. That being said, I feel a lot of Christian books are written by people who feel they've *overcome* something. Maybe they have the answers, and if you just push on a little further everything will be all sunshine and unicorns and leprechauns and whatever else. But that hasn't been my journey, and I'm willing to bet it hasn't been yours either. It doesn't even matter your age, young or old—we're *all* struggling with one thing or another.

I'm calling this *A Voice from the Valley* because that's where I am: somewhere in the valley. I haven't reached the top of the tallest mountain and been able to look down and scoff at everything I've overcome. If we're honest, I don't know if anyone can do that, especially us Christians, but I don't know if any of us are supposed to be able to do that.

John 16:33 says, "In this world you *will* have trouble." We will. It's right there in black and white, thousands of years old, and yet we throw up our arms in the air whenever troubles find us and we ask, "Why do bad things happen to good people?" Life is not easy. Life is hard and unfair and can be bleak and can make you feel so unwanted and so unloved. So where's the hope? In that same verse, Jesus says, "I have overcome the world." And if that weren't true, if there wasn't a loving God up there who gave his only son for you and for me, we'd all be tragically lost, spinning out of control to nowhere on this broken, broken world.

Who's Driving This Thing?

I graduated from grad school with a degree in creative writing. I wrote a lot of sci-fi thrillers and deep realistic dramas and thought I really had a knack for what I was doing. My professors seemed to like my work, as did my peers and my friends. I thought finding a job after graduation was going to be easy. I had a plan. I was going to get a writing related job, maybe do some tutoring, get my sci-fi novel published, get a job teaching in college after that, and then I'd be on my way, all the way to kingdom come.

I was really missing something, though. I've been a Christian for most of my life, since the age of five, but even now I'm still learning what it means to be a Christian. Ready for a brutal awakening? I wasn't, but here we go: my life isn't about me and your life isn't about you. I can't imagine a lot of "amens" after that statement. Our lives are *not* about us. Man, I wanted it all: fame, recognition, a book on a shelf somewhere, to do interviews, money, to be *known*—to be the best. However, that verse isn't in the Bible: "Do what you want to do for you." In fact, it's kind of the opposite, isn't it? "You shall have no other gods before me" (Exodus 20:3). I've heard many sermons about that, where others put money, fame, their spouse, and a million other things in the place of God. For me, I put myself in God's place, and left very little room for him. I was a Christian, yes, but I wanted to call my own shots. I was supposed to let God be the driver in my life, but instead I was sitting next to him, constantly cranking the wheel where *I* wanted to go. The thing with God is, a lot of times, he lets you go where you want to go, and we learn the hard way. *Now*, can I get an amen?

Creeping Crickets

Being my own god made me my own worst enemy. More or less, taking God out of the equation, I was on my own. I had to have an answer for everything. Instead of surrendering my own ambitions and accepting God's will and plan for my life, I exercised controlling and manipulative behaviors. See, without God, I had nothing, but I didn't know that at the time. I had illusions of control, and with those illusions came mild successes which pushed me to continue to control, which all too swiftly became a vicious, vicious cycle.

I've heard it said that Satan's biggest lie is getting people to believe he doesn't exist. It's easy to fight something you can see, but when you're fighting by yourself, not relying on anyone else, let alone God, you're so blind to what's right in front of you. Satan had me right where he wanted me. In the beginning, Satan tricked Adam, saying he could be like God. Satan tricked me the same way, but took a very different and more complex road.

Satan's not stupid. He's not random. He's terrifyingly real and sick and he's *going* to find your weakness and exploit it, either right away or he'll lie and wait. As an example, we used to have this pet frog. We found him in front of our house and decided to keep him for awhile. We'd put crickets in his cage and watch. I thought he'd be on the prowl and have his tongue going like one of those inflatable tube-men, snatching up all those crickets right away, but he didn't. He sat. The crickets would literally be crawling over him, completely oblivious, but he just sat there and waited, and waited, until finally one would climb over his mouth, then—*bam!* Satan is the same way. He's out there waiting for you right now, make no doubt about it, and without God, relying wholly on yourself, you'll suffer the same fate I did, if not worse.

I came crumbling down. Satan had me right where he wanted me. He knew my family's history, knew I had anxiety, knew I was prone to being controlling, and just waited until I had absolutely zero control before he sprung the trap. I believe he's been waiting years for the right moment. He got me and dragged me down to the absolute lowest point of my life, to a point where I was contemplating whether or not life was worth living anymore.

Make no mistake: this isn't about you or me. This is about God, and Satan's doing anything he can to try and make God hurt a little more.

Naked & Afraid

As I sit here and type, I'm reflecting a little bit on my day. It's been the hardest day I've had with anxiety in a couple months. I was called about a job application I filled out and I was immediately filled with dread and self-doubt.

A big cause of my anxiety is perfectionism and control, both of which stemmed from my dysfunctional childhood, and those two traits really don't work all that well together in the workplace. Upon hearing the call, all I could think of was *what if this happens, what if that happens, what if I can't do this, what if I don't know this,* and so on.

We must always be careful what we wish and pray for. I was discouraged when I wasn't getting any callbacks on my applications, then I became utterly fearful and afraid when I finally did.

Life is hard, but God knows that. He knows life is unfair and hard and he knows how it doesn't make any sense to go from one extreme to the other in the matter of a phone call. When it comes to that, when there doesn't seem to be a right answer one way or the other, just remember right now—through God—we're good enough. He's not waiting on us to get a job or get promoted or get married. We don't have to finish first or have a family or own our own business. We don't have to be a year sober, attend church regularly, or volunteer. That doesn't make us enough. We're enough *right now*, right where we are. He made us enough when he died on the cross for us. Just remember that—please remember that: with God, you're enough. Stripped naked and afraid, you're enough.

I Know

My anxiety has been pretty troublesome the past couple days, to a point where it's hard to leave the house. But last night I believe God filled my heart with a little bit of revelation. It deals with comparison vs. connecting.

I had dinner with my brother at a restaurant and I just watched the people working there and I thought, *it's not fair. All of these people are working, doing their jobs, and I can't. It's not fair.* I was comparing myself to them, people I didn't even know.

A lot of times people will say in conversations, "Well, at least we don't have it as bad as so-and-so. Now she has *a lot* going against her." What are we doing? Why are we comparing ourselves to other people? We're not them. We don't know every crevice of their lives. We don't know the depth of their faith. We're all running our own races.

Instead of looking around and seeing what people have and what they can do that we can't, or what they look like, or this and that, just remember everyone is battling *something*. And a lot of times, we're not going to have any idea what that something is.

Yeah, I'm battling anxiety, and it sucks, but those kids working at that restaurant, maybe they're dealing with cancer in the family, or divorce, or addiction to something—everyone has a battle they're fighting. The devil is not tired or taking it easy. He's after every single one of us. We're sheep among wolves out here.

Instead of comparing, when that urge to compare rises, take a step back and pray. See that person you want to compare yourself with and connect with them instead. Pray for them, love on them, and show them you care if you can. We're all battling our own demons. There's no deeper connection between two people than when you can end a sentence with *I know the feeling*. "I feel pain and hurting and loss and I don't know what I'm going to do. I'm so lost." *I know that feeling.* That's connection. That's love. That's what God's family can do.

Run, Rabbit

Paul, in the Bible, is a pretty incredible dude. From Christian killer to Christian to Christian builder. There's a verse of his I love, and it's in 2nd Timothy 4:7, where he says, "I have finished the race." This is a verse we've all heard a hundred times, but there's something specific in it I never noticed until recently.

I've spent so much of my life trying to be the best—the best son, brother, friend, boyfriend, writer, athlete, and so on. You name it. What a rough way to live, constantly trying to be better than somebody, constantly striving to be the best there ever was (a Pokémon reference for you trainers out there).

But Paul was running his own race. We're all running our *own* race. We need to stop comparing, stop struggling, stop fighting, and just run. Don't look left, right, or behind. Pick yourself up when you fall and continue on. Paul says he finished the race. He never says he won it.

Brothers & Sisters

Whenever I take my dog out for a walk, I spend some time talking with God. I breathe in the fresh air and just look up and talk. I really love that, just being able to look up and talk to my creator, my God.

The other day, while doing that, I was going through a lot of anxiety. I came home from my walk and wrote this description of what anxiety is:

> Anxiety is breathing in water,
> trying to see through sand,
> being blasted with air raid sirens,
> rolling in a bed of needles,
> and talking without a voice.

That description may seem extreme, but it doesn't even begin to do all mental disorders justice. Mental disorders are living hells. Absolutely.

If you break a bone, you get a cast, your bones heal. Not with mental disorders. You may get some pills, but they're not going to cure you. Your disorder will remain until you start to get help (counseling or the like), or it may be something you just have to learn to live with to some degree.

Reader, if you have a mental disorder, and you don't think anybody understands your pain, your struggles, your worry, please know I do. Know I feel that pain, and your pain, and I'm sorry, but know you're not alone, I'm not alone—*we're* not alone. As I like to say, we're all in this valley together.

Beggars & Kings

I've been in counseling before, but since starting it up again, the last five months have been pretty spiritually eye-opening for me.

I met with my counselor today, Matt, and we talked about the throne I had built for myself. It was a throne made of awards, recognition, and successes of all kinds. Sitting on my throne, I felt like the king above all kings. Sure, I've failed in my life, but I've done everything I could to add to my throne, to make my throne glamorous and impressive to anyone who'd look at it. At one point, I literally had a wall at home full of my accomplishments, publications, and awards.

Not only was my throne absent of love and humility, but it was an extreme, and it was a throne for myself. There was no space for anyone else, especially God. I was so consumed with myself and with what *I* could achieve, I put God in a box under my bed, then took the wheel and drove like mad.

I didn't get too far. My successes stopped, as they were bound to, and I was left with nothing. This is something so important and something I've heard a million times in church over and over, but I never listened to it until I had no choice: watch out for this world and what it offers.

I was digging a hole that could never be filled, an emptiness that would stay forever. There is no answer to be found in this world, not a permanent one anyway. This world will surely always, *always*, given enough time, leave you lost and cold and all alone.

I've left the throne I've built for myself and have been crawling towards an altar. Matt and I, during a session, talked about Cain and Abel, and how one of their offerings was acceptable to God and the other's wasn't.

I don't know what was on my altar while I was sitting on my throne. Not much. Not much there giving God the glory. Matt challenged me and asked, "Have you ever been willing to put yourself on the altar and ask God to use you for *his* use?"

Wow, going from a "king" to a servant. But what about *my* plans? I had it all figured out. I was the answer man. I was "going places." All until God made me look at my life and honestly evaluate it for the first time.

I had a special moment with God: I went home, turned off all the lights, and spoke to him out loud. I told him I wanted to go where he wanted me to go, and that I wanted to do what he wanted me to do, offering myself wholly and completely to him.

These lives aren't ours. I still forget that and find myself rolling off the altar, but we need to give ourselves to God daily. It's not easy or popular or in-line with society's beliefs, but it's a necessity to give ourselves to God.

It's scary. My throne is what I've known for so long, and there's anxiety when I'm not sitting on it. However, there's also freedom and peace to be found. My throne is gathering dust and my heart aches, but I know all will be well when God has the wheel. Here's my heart, Lord. All will be well.

That Broken Man Is Me

With anxiety and depression and anything else that punches you in the chest, it's easy to get in a mindset where you're looking for a cheap out. It's too easy to get to that place where you can rationalize drinking or drugging or any other kind of addiction (over-eating, sexual impurity, and the like). That's where evil wants us to be, so broken where we need something else to "heal" us, be it ever so temporary.

My family tree has generations of alcoholism. I grew up around it. It hurt me and I'm still feeling the effects of it. I've never been drunk, or even tipsy for that matter, but I've had my addictions, too, most strongly to myself. I needed something to fill a gaping hole in my life. Instead of turning to God and letting him be enough, instead of *surrendering* all to him, I kept on going and tried to fix things myself.

I thought girls, attention, fame, fortune, and being perfect would fill that hole, but all it did was leave me even more broken and lost and scared. There'd be a temporary "fix," but it never lasted. It never does. It never will.

When we feel that hurt, instead of looking for a cheap way out, I want to challenge all of us to look to God instead. I know it sounds cliché, but he's truly the only one that can carry what we're buried under. Drinking, drugging, sexing—that covers the problem, it doesn't deal with it.

In order to find peace with anxiety, depression, and other mental illnesses, we *have* to deal with it. We have to take that step to find help. Help can come in the form of medications, counselors, groups, but the ultimate help and healing comes from God:

> Do you not know? Have you not heard? The Lord is the everlasting God, the creator of the ends of the earth. He will NOT grow tired or weary, and his understanding no one can fathom. He gives strength to the weary and increases the power of the weak. Even youths grow tired and weary, and young men stumble and fall; but those who hope in the Lord will renew their strength. They will soar on wings like eagles; they will run and not grow weary, they will walk and not be faint. (Isaiah 40:28–31)

That's the power we have when we believe and trust in God and surrender everything to him. Life is too much for us. We can't handle it. We can fight against it for a while, but we're going to end up buried underneath it. The only true healing in this world is a renewal of spirit in Jesus Christ. That's it. Everything else is trivial.

Not Overcome

My dad was an alcoholic for most of my life. Growing up in a dysfunctional home is a definite reason for my anxiety and depression, but there are other reasons, also. However, my dad's sober now, truly by the grace of God. I used to pray for his sobriety every night. Writing this, he's been sober for almost six years. Praise God. And now my dad knows about recovery.

I had a pretty severe bout of panic about four months ago. I was in tears, shaking, and with nowhere to turn. I needed help. I was seeing my counselor twice a week, but I needed more. I knew I needed more, but I didn't know what I needed.

I remember I approached my dad and asked him, "What did you do while you were in recovery? How did you make it?" He told me he needed to be around people like him. He needed people in his life who understood exactly what he was going through. He needed a community of recovering alcoholics.

That conversation has really helped guide the direction of my life since. I immediately jumped online and started looking for support groups, and I've found some good ones. I joined some groups on Facebook, where I could ask questions and be part of a community, where its members understood my illnesses because they're ill, too. I also found a group for children of dysfunctional families, and I attend at least one of those meetings a week.

I'm starting to realize healing comes from being pro-active. Sitting and wallowing in our misery is *not* going to help. But I also know how hard it can be to motivate yourself to get out of the house when you're full of anxiety and dread.

I want to challenge all of you to find a support group—people who know *exactly* what you're going through. Trust me, they're out there. There's no greater feeling than when you're describing how horrible and lost you feel, and someone else says, "I've been there, too."

God created other people just like us so we can be there as a community of believers for one another. "If one falls down, his friend can help him up . . . though one may be overpowered, two can defend themselves. A cord of three strands is not quickly broken" (Ecclesiastes 4:10a and 12).

Pain the Devil

I'm not a theology major, I don't know Greek, I can't recite all twelve disciples, but I have heard scholars say the book of Job is one of the oldest in the Bible, if not *the* oldest. Why is that significant to me now, amidst everything else? Well, I'm glad you asked.

Here's this guy, Job, writing before he knew much. He may have heard stories about God's faithfulness, but he didn't have the Bible, let alone any books of the Bible. Yet, his relationship and trust in God was absolutely unshakeable.

Job lost so much, more than I can even imagine losing, and he still remained faithful to God. Although it may be easy to say Job made it out okay, he didn't know how it was going to end at the time.

Here we are, centuries later, with the Bible and mountains of other inspirational works, and yet we still wonder if God's got our back. *Job had none of it!* But, when asked by his friends to curse out God, Job said, "God has made my heart faint; the almighty has terrified me. Yet I am not silenced by the darkness, by the thick darkness that covers my face" (Job 23:16–17). Job lost his livestock, was covered in open wounds, and even lost his children, yet he trusted God. Later on, while his buddies were still trying to get him to turn against God, Job said, "Until I die, I will not deny my integrity" (27:5).

Man, that's faith. How quick I've turned against God, even wondering if he knows what I'm going through down here. I lose faith at times, but what a great reminder Job gives us, to remain faithful through all. We may not like it, however, we can find peace in God knowing all is under his control. Nothing goes unnoticed.

No tear is lost. Let's pray to have half of Job's faith, a faith so deep he was able to say, "Though he slay me, yet will I hope in him" (13:15).

We're going through some of the hardest trials on earth, but God has not forgotten about us. Let's halt ourselves from turning our backs on God, and instead praise him—he knows the number of hairs on our heads (Luke 12:7).

The devil hates seeing Christians going through hell, praising God. So, let's pain the devil a bit . . . he's sure hurt us enough.

Babel

Sometimes it's hard to see God, don't get me wrong. Concrete everywhere, steel, glass. Don't even turn on the news. There's always so much going on in our lives (work, family, money), we constantly pass what's so familiar, but what's so rich in God's goodness.

Our visible sky doesn't change much, and hasn't changed much since the beginning of time. The ground is constantly changing, a new road here, a growing skyscraper over there, but the sky almost remains untouched by man.

The sky is endless and beautiful and God's. Whenever you need a reminder of God and where he is, just look up. See him in the sun. See him in the clouds. See him in the moon and stars (if you haven't already, check out *Indescribable* by Louie Giglio).

Take a moment to look up and breathe and know you're looking up and seeing what David saw, what Paul saw, what Jesus saw.

God may seem distant at times, but he's always right with us, even inside of us. To remember that, just look up. He sees you, too.

You

A woman in one of my support groups said something a couple weeks ago that's still resonating with me now. What she said was so sweet and simple, yet something that's been hard for me to do, and maybe you can relate.

She said, "Be quick to pat yourself on the back."

I come from a place where everything had to be perfect: everything had to look perfect, we had to act perfect, and to the outside world everything inside was perfect. That's a high standard to keep as a young kid, let alone someone in high school, college, and beyond.

I didn't know it or recognize it at the time, but I was a perfectionist. I was always striving for that next achievement, that next gold star. But my successes never lasted. After one, I was immediately thinking of the next one. I never stopped and enjoyed what I had.

When my counselor and I discussed my perfectionism for the first time, I was literally sick to my stomach. I had gotten everything so mixed up. It's impossible to be perfect. Did you know that? And who would want to be? There's only one perfect person that ever walked this earth and we took him and crucified him.

God *never* calls us to be perfect. That's not a commandment. He knows we're going to screw up and that's why he sent Jesus.

Coming down from my perfectionist thinking has been the cause of so much anxiety and depression. It's hard to let myself fail and let myself be.

I have a praise deficit. At times, I still look for appreciation and praise from people who I know won't—or can't—give it to me. I feel I have to be this perfect son, brother, friend, etc. I feel like I have to please everybody—a people-pleaser.

But what about us? We surrender our own idea of self to try and be something for somebody else. But what does the Bible say? In Matthew 22:39 it says, "Love your neighbor as *yourself*."

We have to love ourselves. Isn't that something so simple, yet so hard? Why do we have to be so hard on ourselves? A lot of times we're the cause of our own anxieties and depressions. What if we let go a little bit, showed ourselves some grace, and just patted ourselves on the back?

I was driving to one of my meetings and I was thinking about what that woman said, about patting ourselves on the back (which is now written in permanent marker on my wall, right above my computer). Earlier that day I had tried to seek praise from someone else, and they didn't give it to me. I felt defeated and shamed and anxious. Then I remembered those words: *be quick to pat yourself on the back.*

Out loud, I said, "I'm proud of you, Tim. You're working really hard. I'm proud of you, buddy." I got so emotional in that moment. Perfectionism was losing its grip as I applauded myself right where I was. I didn't win an award or get a job or make a payment on anything, but I was content in that moment, right where I was.

Accept who you are and where you are, right now. See the hard work you're doing. See your struggles and see how you live in spite of them.

Darkness, My Old Friend

There was a day, a few months back now, when I just couldn't take it anymore. I was home alone and anxiety was burning inside me uncontrollably. I was trembling, my mind was racing, my breaths were short. The medication wasn't helping. All I wanted to do was scream.

That's when I had the most honest conversation of my life, and it was with God. Tears were gushing down my face as I cried out to God:

Don't you see me? Don't you see what I'm going through down here? Do something! Do something! Why don't you help me? Can't you see I need you? Can't you see I'm not going to make it? Help me! God, help me!

I went on like that for about fifteen minutes. I spoke to God in the most honest way I had ever spoken to anyone. I let him know I wasn't happy. I let him know I didn't like his plan for me right then. I let him know I felt lost and scared and felt abandoned by him.

I was never taught to speak to God like that—it just happened. But after I got it all out, I felt a sense of relief. I felt *heard*.

I feel there's an unwritten rule that Christians can't get angry or upset with God, and that's absolutely false. We're not always in a state of happiness, and that's okay. It's okay to not be okay.

Just look at David in Psalm 88:

- "You have put me in the lowest pit, in the darkest depths" (verse 6).
- "Why, O Lord, do you reject me and hide your face from me?" (verse 14).
- "The darkness is my closest friend" (verse 18b).

God can take what we dish out. He can handle our grief. He's not going to run away and be hurt every time we don't like going through pain.

Just whenever you're angry with God, don't sin (Ephesians 4:26). Don't belittle God or mock him or swear against him. Keep reverence, but know it's okay to show him your true feelings.

David was a man after God's own heart. He praised God when life was good, and he cried out when life was bad. And that's okay.

Don't sugarcoat it for God, either. He knows how you're feeling, so just get it out. Cry out to him—especially him. Some of the closest people to you may not be able to listen to (or handle) your pain, but God *can*, and he always has an ear ready for you.

Our God

But does God get it? Does he know our pain? Does he see us down here, with our hands covering our faces, tears streaming through our fingers, and really *know* our pain? Does he *know* what we're going through?

If he didn't, how could he truly help us? I know there are people in all of our lives that we've tried talking to about our illnesses. We've tried explaining our anxieties and depressions and fears and doubts, and they just don't get it. A lot of them end up giving terrible advice, telling you to just shrug it off and push on. We need a God who understands what it means to be utterly and hopelessly human, and ours does.

Jesus walked among us. He wept when his friend Lazarus died. He was angry when his "house" was turned into a flea market. He was completely crushed and heart-broken on the cross, so much so he cried out, "My God, why have you forsaken me?"

(Mark 15:34b) Our God knows our pain, and that's why we can trust him with it.

I needed that reassurance when my anxiety was at its worst, and there was a part of scripture I was drawn towards, and that's when Jesus was praying in Gethsemane, just hours before his death. Jesus knew what was coming. He knew the pain and sorrow that was to come. So he prayed. And he prayed hard. In scripture, it says, "And being in anguish, he prayed more earnestly, and his sweat was like drops of blood falling to the ground" (Luke 22:44).

That's our God. In that moment, I can't imagine the anxieties and fears and helplessness he felt. He was about to be thrown to the wolves for you and for me.

God knows our pains. He knows what it's like to feel all alone. He knows what it's like when you feel like this world is coming down on you. He knows what it's like when you feel like nobody understands you.

He *knows*, and he feels your pain, and it'll be safe with him.

The Moment of Surrender

I'm at a point where I feel overwhelmed: I've sent out over fifty job applications with little to no responses, I'm having relationship troubles, I have student loans due with no money to pay them, and throw in anxiety and depression and I've got myself a pretty frothy, nasty cocktail.

But for myself, and for you, let's never forget we can ask for help when we need it. Growing up in a dysfunctional household, I had to become independent early on, and that's a trait I still carry with me. However, it's not always an admirable trait.

The world tells us to be independent, to look out for number one, and that there's no mountain we can't climb alone.

How does that work when we were made to be dependent beings? God tells us to look to him, to trust him, to put him first. The world and God don't see eye-to-eye here. One is right and one is wrong.

We *need* God and we need other believers. We need prayer. We need an open dialogue with God, praising his plan for us, but also pleading for help and guidance. We need other Christians to pray for us. Sometimes we just need to vent to somebody we can trust. We need each other, no matter what the ads say.

I know it's hard to ask for help. My anxiety rises every time I have to ask. But we're never going to make it by ourselves. We need to surrender the grip we think we have on our lives.

Surrender is a word covered with the stigma of weakness. I want to change that and have it become a word covered with trust and honesty. When we surrender our fears to God, and place our wills and our lives in his care, that's not weakness—that's a trust that the God who created this world and died for us is still there, still listening, and still cares more than we'll ever know.

We need to stop standing, pretending we have it all figured out, and just collapse before him in an utter and sweet surrender. We need to trust that he has our backs. Ask him, trust him, and believe him when he says, "Look at the birds of the air; they do not sow or reap or store away in barns, and yet your heavenly father feeds them. Are you not much more valuable than they?" (Matthew 6:26)

Let's depend on God and let's depend on each other. We have our valleys, but that's what binds us together—our struggles. Let's raise our voices in prayer to God for each other, and for ourselves. Be willing to surrender. Be willing to let go and trust. Be willing to try.

Only Human

All right, let's dig deep for a second. I'm just going to throw this out there (let it sink in for a moment): who can you cut out of your life?

How was that? Did the face of somebody appear? Did you feel anything inside? Are you trying to figure out if you're allowed to cut people out of your life?

In one of my support groups, a gentleman was talking about his deceased, dysfunctional father and he made a pretty clear distinction. He said, "I didn't like my dad, but I loved him." Certainly there *is* a difference.

We are called to love, absolutely. But you know what we're not called to do? Be friends with everyone we come across. Some people don't fit our personalities, and that's okay! For me, I'm more of a laid-back, flip on a movie, and take it easy kind of guy. I wouldn't make a good friend to someone who has to go out and socialize every night. That's just not who I am.

But it goes deeper, too. There are people we just need to let go of. They're toxic. They're manipulative. They are all about themselves and not about you. Your healing comes second to them, or maybe even last. I'm sure all of you know exactly what I'm saying here. We are dealing with some of life's hardest challenges and the last thing we need is someone in our lives who's negative, draining, and selfish.

Let's look at Mark 6:31 and 32:

> Because so many people were coming and going that they did not even have a chance to eat, he [Jesus] said to them, 'Come with me by yourselves to a quiet place and get some rest.' So they went away by themselves in a boat to a solitary place.

The disciples needed a break. They were worn out. And us? We're only human. There are just people that, no matter what you do, it'll never be enough. They'll continue to be miserable, angry people. You can bend over backwards for these people until you snap in two and it'll still make no difference to them. We need to rest. We need to take time for ourselves. And that's okay.

I have a toxic relationship with someone. Toxic to its core. I've been "friends" with her for about ten years and our friendship is ridiculous. I'm the one that's always reaching out. I'm the one that's always asking how she's doing and how I can help her. I'm the one always trying to get together and see her. What am I doing? I need to step back and just let it go. Relationships/friendships are give and take. If you see one of your relationships is out of balance, action needs to be taken.

Let him go. Let her go. Let them go. Let it go.

We can love these people and pray for these people, but we do not need to sacrifice ourselves and our sanity for them. Some of us have terrible critics—maybe even family members. It seems whatever we do is never enough for them. Let them go. Bye-bye.

It's time to end the people-pleasing and begin recovery. However, there are great people in your life, also, and thank God for them. They're with you no matter what. What a blessing they are.

But those that are sapping your strength, energy, happiness, and making you worse off, filling you with dread, stress, anxiety, and even more depression—it's okay to let them go and break away and take a breath far from them.

We are dealing with enough and Jesus knows we need rest, too.

Of Clay

For me, I know there are times when I'm ashamed of my anxiety. I can get embarrassed when I'm anxious, and instead of dealing with the issue, I'll try to hide it. I'll even try to hide my medication. Instead of being outright that I have to take meds, I'll excuse myself or quickly take a pill with a sip of Dr. Pepper hoping no one will notice. There are times when I'll feel humiliated I have to use the bathroom because my bowels will be acting up due to my internal stress. Maybe you can relate?

It's important to remember, though, that we *are* fearfully and wonderfully made by our God (Psalm 139:14a). Although we may not be where we want to be in our recovery or with our lives or with our illnesses, it doesn't change the fact God created us wonderfully. We are masterpieces. We are *exactly* the way we're supposed to be.

I know it might sound kind of cliché, but what if we started to accept ourselves? What if we didn't hide our anxieties from our families and friends? What if we tried to trust someone close to us?

Granted, some people won't get it or understand it, and some might even ignore it or ridicule it, so we need to be careful with who we trust and open up our stories to. And from experience, I know there are no greater people who understand mental illness than those with mental illness themselves.

I remember I had to email my boss once, when I was really sick with anxiety and couldn't work. I told her straight up I had an anxiety issue I was dealing with and didn't know when I would be back to work. She emailed me back and told me she understood completely, because she had an anxiety issue, too.

That won't be the case every time, but you never know. Some people will get it and some won't. My bottom line here is that we shouldn't feel we have to hide it. People don't hide taking pain pills or cough medicine, so why should we hide our illnesses, too?

We're sick, but that's okay. Taking pills is okay. Taking a day for yourself, away from work, is okay. Telling your brother or sister or mom or dad or best friend or close friend about your illness is *okay*! I've been talking more and more about my anxiety with my family, and when I talk it feels like a burden is being lifted. We can't keep stuffing everything in.

If there's no one you can think of who would understand your story or show you grace, find an online anxiety/depression/mental illness group. Those are great places to talk and discuss and feel heard.

It's okay to be who you are, so be that person. You are wonderfully made by the king of kings.

The "Can-Do" Attitude

This next vignette (I don't like the word "vignette," it sounds kind of pretentious, but it's a word I learned in my fifty-thousand dollar school loan grad school, so I might as well use it) came as inspiration from the walls in my room.

What were going through with our mental illnesses is not easy. There are days when it feels like we're living in Hell. At times, these lives are painful, coarse, tragic, and seemingly hopeless. Am I connecting with anybody yet?

Granted, there are times when life seems refreshing, when we feel good, when we feel like we can make it and survive and do this thing called life. But I know the feeling after that, too, when the glow fades and we end up back in a dark, humbling, discouraging place. A lot of people use the term "roller-coaster" to describe mental illness and I couldn't agree more. It's a roller-coaster with ups and downs, sharp turns, and even hard brakes.

That's where my walls come in. My room walls are covered with papers: papers with inspirational quotes, Biblical truths/verses, and reminders of hope. Here are just a few:

- Put God First
- Let Go & Let God
- Progress, not Perfection
- Surrender & Accept
- God says you're able to bear what you're going through
- Just let God be Enough

Overall, I have seventy-three papers posted on my walls. I can barely see the paint. And why? Because I need seventy-three reminders every day that I can make it, I can do it, and with God nothing is impossible.

We need constant encouragement because we don't know what's coming next. None of us do. We need to be lifted up and encouraged before we ever step foot out of our rooms in the morning. That's not something we can depend on the outside world for.

We can do this. Even if it takes constant reminders, like little notes we write ourselves to read at lunch every day, we can do this. We just have to get creative. Don't be afraid to mess up your walls, take sticky notes with you, or haul your Bible around for a couple quick verse readings throughout the day.

Let's just remind ourselves we can do this. We got this.

Mission Control

I started my truck the other day and my check-engine light went on. Immediately my mind went worst-case-scenario: *I can't afford to fix anything. What if I need a new vehicle? How am I going to get places? This is so unfair.*

A Voice from the Valley

The next day, I started my truck and the check-engine light didn't come on, and hasn't come on since.

I think it's easy with mental illness to automatically assume the worst. A number you don't know calls you—*who is it? Did something terrible happen?* Your boss asks to see you—*what did I screw up? I'm getting fired.* Your doctor wants to schedule another appointment—*what did he find? Is it cancer?*

It's too easy to go down the rabbit-hole and assume extremes. It's too easy to lose hope and expect the worst. It's too easy to count ourselves out.

Remember this, though—you're still here. If you're reading this, you've survived every single one of your worst days. With God, we're going to survive. Instead of going worst-case-scenario with everything, we need to give it over to God immediately. *God, I'm worried there may be something wrong with my vehicle. You know my situation. I give it over to you.*

In saying words like that—*boom!*—you're no longer in control. God's got it and he can handle it.

Moving forward, let's trust him with *everything*, and admit we can't do it anymore by ourselves.

To Find Peace & Rest

What are our expectations based on? Who, or what, are we comparing ourselves to? "Well look at Joe Nobody down the street. He doesn't deal with depression. He's doing fine. Why can't I do fine?" Or are we watching too much TV? "Look at all those beautiful people. Why can't I be beautiful like them?" Or are we listening to family and friends who really don't have our best interests at heart? Do they say things like, "Why don't you just toughen up and get over it?" Or, "Stop being lazy. You're a grown man. Start acting like it."

We are constantly—*constantly*—getting bombarded with impossible expectations. To say it flat out: we cannot compare ourselves to others. If we do that, we will never find contentment.

How much anxiety, depression, and OCD has been caused by trying to be something/someone we're not? *I have to look like her. I have to act like him. I have to make my parents happy. I have to be a manager. I have to be married by the time I'm thirty. I have to have a house in that neighborhood and drive that car and wear those kinds of clothes.* We need to stop it already and just let all of that fall off!

Imagine, just for a moment, wearing a heavy backpack and walking with it for miles. It starts to strain your back and the straps dig into your shoulders and you're sweating—it's literally weighing you down. Now imagine that feeling of refreshment when you let the backpack roll down your arms and onto the ground. That's what we need to do with these worldly ideas and expectations. If we try to meet all of them, we'll never be content. It'll always be about what's next and completely ignoring the moment.

The only true happiness (and lasting happiness) on this earth comes from God. It's not popular, it's not going to turn a lot of heads, but you'll never feel better than when you truly let all those false expectations go, like that backpack off your shoulders.

For me, success was winning a Pulitzer. Success was making more money than anyone else in my family and never having to ask for help. Success was getting tenure at a college. Success was making *everyone* proud. Are some of those goals a bit extreme? Absolutely. And more than that, I was missing something huge: success is not external, it's internal.

- "But the fruit of the Spirit is love, joy, peace, patience, kindness, goodness, faithfulness, gentleness, and self-control. Against such things there is no law" (Galatians 5:22–23).
- "So the last will be first, and the first will be last" (Matthew 20:16).
- "If anyone would come after me, he must deny himself and take up his cross and follow me. For whoever wants to save his life will lose it, but whoever loses his life for me will find it. What good will it be for a man if he gains the whole world, yet forfeits his soul?" (Matthew 16:24–26)

These verses are radical. And I don't want to come at this being condescending to anyone, because I still struggle with this and forget it: success is not contentment—contentment is success.

The apostles didn't have much. Paul didn't have much. John the Baptist didn't have much. But they all found peace, didn't they? Peace in Jesus.

When we become Christians, we are bathed in the Holy Spirit. We are transformed and renewed. And I'll say it again—it is not easy being a Christian in this world. We are bombarded and battered and this world is trying to wrap its arms around us and drag us down to its level.

Peace is found in God. It's so hard to accept, because it's not the norm. The world is preaching one thing and Jesus is saying another. He says, "Come to me, all you who are weary and burdened, and I will give you rest" (Matthew 11:28). Rest. Let that word sink in.

So much of my anxiety has come from fighting for achievements and relevance and trying to be perfect. I put God behind all of that. I didn't deny myself and I was willing to sacrifice my own soul for success. I wanted to be first.

God doesn't want our money or our name to be in lights or our trophies and gold medals. You know what he wants? He wants us—he wants you.

Someone Tell Me Why

I know you've asked this question, and I've personally probably asked it a hundred times (if not more than that), and here's the question: why?

Why all the pain? Why all the sadness? Why all the confusion? Why can't I do this or that or just be *normal*?

It's a painful question to ask. Why anxiety, depression, OCD, and the others? And to be honest, there's not an easy answer. While we only see a small portion of our lives, God sees the bigger picture.

For starters, let's look at Romans 9:20–21:

> But who are you, O man, to talk back to God? "Shall what is formed say to him who formed it, 'Why did you make me like this?'" Does not the potter have the right to make out of the same lump of clay some pottery for noble purposes and some for common use?

This verse says a lot, but I want to point out something very specific here: we are formed and we are made. We don't roll off an assembly line. We're not haphazardly thrown together. We're not accidents and God is *not* a kid with an ant farm.

When we were created, God took his time with us. When I was doing my undergrad, I took a pottery class to fill an elective, and making pottery (correctly) is truly an art—something I never came close to mastering; each of my clay salad bowls weighed about six pounds.

The potter sits at a wheel and delicately shapes the clay in their hands, forming it tall, wide, short, skinny—the possibilities are really endless. Some pots have holes in them. Some have decorations and etchings. Some can be sat on. Others hold paperclips. Take heart here and know God had a specific plan when he created you.

God didn't fall asleep at the wheel and that's how we ended up with our mental illnesses. He didn't look down at us and go, "Oh boy, I turned away for a second to get the muffins out of the oven, and *boom*—they ended up with depression. I got to stop doing that." We were made the ways we are for a reason. That's a biblical truth. You're also a male/female for a reason, grew up in the house you did for a reason, the part of the world you did for a reason, and this time in history for a reason (just to name a few of the reasons). You *have* a purpose. I have a purpose. Everyone has a purpose. Is it painful? At times, absolutely. Is it horrible? At times, absolutely. Is it fair? At times, definitely not. However, what Satan wants to burn you down with, you can rise above and use for good.

For me, I'm writing this. In spite of my anxieties, I'm writing this, hoping to reach others—maybe just one other—and let that person know they're not crazy and they're not alone. For you, maybe it's connecting with a friend at school, or work, or your kids—connecting with them and bonding with them and showing them it's okay and that they're not alone. No one is ever alone. Ever!

The other point I want to make here is another hard one to grasp, but I've found it to be completely true in my life: my anxieties and my depressions have driven me straight into the arms of my God. They've taught me I have no control over my life, they've taught me life is unfair, and they've also taught me to turn to my God and trust him.

There are times when you *feel* alone, but remember you're not. God's there, sitting right next to you. He's got his hand on your shoulder.

There are still times when I question my anxiety, I'll admit that, but I know God has a plan for it and for me—God has promised me plans of hope and a future (Jeremiah 29:11).

Before my anxiety kicked into high gear again, God was sitting in the passenger seat. But when my anxiety got the best of me, I had nowhere else to turn. I turned to God and he accepted me with open arms.

The devil hates that. He wants us to turn elsewhere. He wants to turn our sorrows into a train wreck. But I want to challenge you to trust God instead. Let your weaknesses transform you, and let them renew your faith in God and his awesome power. God will *never* leave you or forsake you (Deuteronomy 31:6).

One more challenge for tonight, for when you go to bed: when you're praying, thank God for the way you are. Thank him for his design and his plan. Thank him for always being there. And thank him that he'll never let go.

In one of recovery meetings, a gentleman named Mark stood and said, "I'm thankful for my struggle, because I know the God I know now because of it."

Spitting Tar

I'm a great liar. For so long I would say, "I'm a terrible liar. You can always tell when I'm lying." And that was a lie in itself.

I built up a wall around myself. I didn't let anyone in. It was me and the walls around me. As far as anyone was concerned, I was happy, healthy, and content with my life, living it to its fullest. Inside the walls, though, I was scared, lonely, and anxious to my core.

When my anxiety was at a peak, about six months ago now, I came clean on Facebook. I told everyone I had been dealing with anxiety my entire life and that I would appreciate any prayers they could share. I was desperate for help. One of my old friends (who I used to sit next to in my classes, who I used to go out to lunch with, who I used to hang out with) messaged me and said, "I had no idea you had anxiety. You're always so calm and laid-back."

I was great at hiding. Granted, there are times when I still try to hide my anxiety (mostly because I'm too proud at moments), but we need to get all of those fears/doubts/and other thoughts out. We need an outlet.

Some of my outlets include playing/singing songs, some Christian, some not. I also write/journal. I go to support groups and counseling. I'm getting better at talking with my family and friends. I also spend a lot of time in prayer and conversation with God.

We all *need* outlets. For example, David wrote poetry and played the harp. Before any of my outlets, I bottled everything up. It led to stomach issues, bowel issues, and anxiety so bad I ended up in the emergency room. We can't hold on to all this blackness. It's sticky as tar and weighs us down. We need to purge ourselves of it and let it go.

There's fear in letting go, I know. It can be scary at first to talk with family, friends, or counselors/therapists, especially if you've never talked about yourself so personally before. Anxiety may rise, initially, but you're taking a step, a healthy, small first step on a journey with millions of steps to follow. Shed a little here and a little there. Spit out that tar. Let it go.

For me, the walls needed to come down, brick by brick. I still have some pieces standing, but I'm working on it, and it's okay that it takes time.

And again, please know you're not alone. There are literally millions of others dealing with the same issues and thoughts. We're all stuffing our thoughts and feelings together. Maybe we can all flush them out together, too.

Also, please remember God's right there: "For I am the Lord, your God, who takes hold of your right hand and says to you, Do not fear; I will help you" (Isaiah 41:13). Your daddy's got your hand and he's ready to listen. Do you have anything you want to tell him?

Dive, Dive

These next couple sections here, I want to go deep. It's not necessarily going to be easy, but it's going to be real, and it's when you're real that you connect with people the most.

I had really bad anxiety early in my twenties. My buddy and I were taking a road trip to Nashville, to visit my sister. My anxiety in the car was off the charts. I didn't know how to cope with what I was dealing with. My medications didn't seem to be working. But along the way I found something to help dull that anxious, racing mind: alcohol.

Now, I wouldn't get plastered or anything like that, but I'd mix my Xanax with a beer or two, in hopes to feel a little lighter, a little less attached. Alcoholism runs in my family. Knowing that, I still took the risk of drinking when I could, to try and feel some relief.

Truly, even up until this point of me writing, right now, it's only by the grace of God I haven't turned wholly to drugs or alcohol myself. In a way they "help," right? They help create some distance, help you forget, even might help you have a little bit of fun. However, when you take a risk like that, you're just asking for more pain and more problems down the road.

In Proverbs 6:27 and 28, we're asked, "Can a man scoop fire into his lap without his clothes being burned? Can a man walk on hot coals without his feet being scorched?" It's not just drugs or alcohol either. To dull that anxiety or depression, or to forget any of our problems, we could turn to sex, overeating, overspending—*any* addiction. Addiction is a way to focus our thinking on something other than the problem.

What we're all dealing with is not easy, but we need to be stronger than our problems. Just recently I've had a hankering for a beer. A single beer. Came out of nowhere. I felt if I had a beer, I'd feel a little better. That's not coming from God. That's coming from the devil and he's a liar and he wants me to give up and fall flat on my face.

Things that numb us don't help us: drugs, alcohol, sex, overeating, etc. These lead to more problems. In my support groups, I've heard them all. In my own life, I've seen the price that's had to be paid, and continues to be paid.

Remember, God has overcome this world. We need to rely on him every second of every day. A friend in college once told me, "An idle mind is the devil's playground." Watch out for him lurking in your weaknesses. He knows them and he's just waiting for the right time to exploit them.

What do you do if you need help? If you feel tempted? If you feel there's an easier way out? Get on those knees and wear out that carpet. Pray. Give it all to God. And talk to someone. Get connected in a group, even if it's online, and just talk to someone. Ask someone to pray for you, or with you. Remember, you're not alone dealing with *anything*. You're not going through anything no one else has ever gone through. We're brothers and sisters in Christ and we need to help one another out of love.

And know, whoever you are, that I'm praying for you right now:

God, I ask you to be with my family that's in the valley. I know what it feels like to think you're all alone and nobody understands you. Please bless them with *your* peace and *your* hope and *your* rest. Let them feel your presence, for you are God and you are good. Amen.

Twenty Thousand Leagues Under

This is the one I've been dreading writing for a while. This is the bottom. Rock bottom. It's hard to talk about, but I'm praying God will bless me with the right words.

A Voice from the Valley

I call it "Dark Thursday." It was a couple weeks after my anxiety came back, when I was at an ultimate low. It was during a time where my psychiatrist and I discussed upping my medication, which I was doing, and I was warned there could be some extreme side-effects. I also didn't have a very high opinion of myself at the time: *Why are you going through anxiety again? Aren't you stronger than this? You're never going to get better.* It was the perfect storm.

I was in my bed and it was maybe around seven or eight at night. I remember I had my blinds closed, but I could still see the dark blue from outside. I also remember the only thought going through my mind: you can end this.

I've never had serious thoughts like that in my life. I'm a pretty light-hearted person (for the most part), but nevertheless, the thought kept repeating over and over in my head. The longer I sat there, the more the thought repeated. I was (bleeping) terrified.

I eventually called my dad into the room, told him the thoughts I was having, and gave him my handgun to hold onto. I called my psychiatrist the following day and told him what was going on. He described it as my mind being in desperation-mode. What a perfect phrase to describe it. I was desperate. To me, my life was absolutely out-of-control. My plans were gone. My future was in jeopardy. I had no idea what I was going to do. I didn't think I had the strength to take one more step.

Then there were more thoughts: get in the car, get on the highway, pull over, then jump into traffic. My own mind was against me. It was like my best friend turning and stabbing me in the front. I had no idea what to do. I was lost in the deepest pit of the valley.

During all of that chaos, I continued to journal. This is a blurb from one of the pages:

Will it ever get better? I don't want to be a financial burden. I don't want to be this way anymore. Anxiety everywhere.

At the time, I even wrote a poem about it:

> It's now or never, 'cause they're digging in
> cracked my shell, spilled my sin.
> They are the wolves and I'm the sheep.
> They're closing my eyes, here comes the big sleep.

Never easy, just look at my past
and with this breath, almost my last—
Father God, I need you.
Father God, where are you?

It was the darkest and lowest point of my life, and I know some of you know *exactly* what I'm talking about. I was at my edge. I didn't see the future—at all. I saw nothing but a way out, seemingly the only thing I thought I could control.

But I'm still here. Praise God, I'm still here. I surrounded myself with family. I never allowed myself to be home alone. I stopped driving. I did everything I could think of to try and protect myself, because my own thoughts were betraying me.

Inside, I was telling myself I was worthless, weak, and never going to get better. But that's not what the Bible says. The Bible says in Romans 8:37, "In all these things we are more than conquerors through him who loved us." We are *conquerors*. We are fighters. We are warriors. Through Christ, there is nothing we can't handle.

I had lost sight of that. I couldn't see anything. Just hopelessness.

But I'm still here. Amen and praise God. Anxiety, depression, PTSD, addictions—they're killers. They are vicious weapons the enemy uses to confuse and break us. The enemy absolutely broke me and left me for dead, but that's where I reached out for God and he found me.

If you're having dark thoughts, there are things you can do. You're not out of options. Tell someone—family, friends, church goers, people in support groups. Somebody you trust *needs* to know. If it's an emergency, call the hotline (800-273-8255) or 911. There's help out there, but you have to humble yourself to a point where you can allow yourself to ask for it.

Some of the signs I've taped around my room read:

- Think Positive
- God *has* a purpose for you
- Lift your hands up above the darkness
- God *Loves* You!!!

A Voice from the Valley

I still need those reminders on a daily basis. This life is not easy, and it hurts at times, and it can bring you to the edge, but surrender to God. Give everything to him. Not just some things. *Everything.* Let him handle it. That's one of the reasons I'm sitting here right now. I learned to let God have my life, one day at a time.

Going through that major spell of depression, I watched a lot of sermons online for inspiration. I came across one by Louie Giglio called "Symphony." Summarizing part of it, Louie talks about his struggle with anxiety and depression. Hearing a man of God talking about depression brought so much hope to my heart. Louie let me know it was okay, and that I wasn't alone.

Reader, I don't know your story specifically, but I *know* your story. I lived my own version of it. Don't think for one second you're alone, and don't think for one second you're crazy. Through God, and to him be all the glory, I was able to get up out of that pit. Doctors, counselors, family, friends, and support groups, they all helped me, but God grabbed me and raised me and set me down under the moonlight. He did it for me and he can do it for you. Don't hesitate to ask him for help, and don't hesitate to ask others.

You can do it—we can all do it. This valley is like nothing else out there, and there are some extremely dark places in it, but already I'm making the devil mad by saying, "Praise God, he saved me." He's ready to save you, too.

Amazing Love

All right, let's take a little breather here. We've been going through some heavy stuff the last couple pages and I just want to take a moment, right now, to remind you that you are a son/daughter of the king of kings and Lord of lords. He is the beginning and the end, the lion of Judah, and he's got your back.

It doesn't matter what you've done in your life, okay? Jesus Christ still loves you. Whenever you think you're screwing up, or that you're not worth the lint in your pockets, just take a moment, see the cross, and see the creator of all things on it, and he was on it because he loves you, and he continues to love you. He knew, before this world was formed, that if he created this world, he would have to die for it, and he did it anyway. Why? Because he wants a relationship with you based on love, and he's already shown how deep his love is.

Just remember who your true father is. Anxiety, depression, and the rest can't even stand in the presence of our God. Every knee will bow and every tongue will confess that he is Lord.

If you haven't given him your heart yet, consider it now. There's no true healing without him. There's no true peace without him. He is God and he is good and he loves you. *You.* He loves you—now—just the way you are. You don't have to earn his love. It's already here and for the taking. All he wants is your heart.

"But my heart's broke. You don't know who I am or what I've done."

You're right. I don't know. That's between you and God. All I know is that Paul, one of the strongest Christians of all time, once a murderer of Christians, wrote, "Christ Jesus came into this world to save sinners of whom I am *the worst*" (1 Timothy 1:15b).

Jesus didn't come to save some and not others. He came to save all, no matter how bad you think you've muddied your life.

We don't have to work for God. He already did the work. All we have to do is ask him to come into our hearts and give him our hearts wholly, holding nothing back. When we take him, we sacrifice ourselves and our egos, and *that* is enough, and that is all he requires. We have a beautiful, awesome Savior.

Isaac on the Altar

We're getting close to the end of our time together. Thinking and weighing on that, I want to propose a question to you, and it's really quite simple, yet it's so important: what can *you* offer?

And don't say "nothing," because that's not the right answer. I believe everyone can offer *something*. For more on this, you can read 1 Corinthians 12:12–31, where Paul discusses the Body of Christ and how there are many parts to this body. I just want to read a short part here: "If the whole body were an eye, where would the sense of hearing be? If the whole body were an ear, where would the sense of smell be? But in fact God has arranged the parts in the body, every one of them, just as he wanted them to be" (verses 17 and 18).

We, as Christians, all make up a part of this body. You are a crucial part of this body—make no mistake about that. The body is a lesser place without *you*! No one can take your spot. Your spot was designed for you to fill, and only you. Now, I want to ask again: what can you offer?

For me, it's taken years to find just part of an answer. My anxiety crippled me for awhile. I was scared to even leave the house, so I started a Facebook page to connect with others dealing with the same illnesses, but keeping God in the center. Taking to mind my circumstances, I found a way to offer my gifts and talents. That's an offering: offering time, an ear, and advice.

I feel that question comes with a lot of weight, right? *What can you offer?* If you grew up in a church, I feel that question almost implies that if you don't fly half-way across the world and become a missionary you're a bad Christian, and that is simply not the case. You know what's an offering? Saying a prayer. It sounds so simple and doable, but that's an offering. You can bring that to the table. You can be a prayer warrior. You can text your friends and ask how you can pray for them. You can pray for the people in-line behind you at the grocery store. You can pray for your country.

There are literally countless ways you can offer yourself and be used by God, however, we can only be used if we allow ourselves to be. We have to have an open heart and an open mind. Going back to an earlier illustration, we have to be willing to put ourselves on the altar and ask God, "How do you want me to serve?"

For some of us, maybe we can donate money. For others, maybe we can volunteer. I understand mental illness can be terrifying and that it can limit us. Some of us are terrified to drive, let alone fly. So don't complicate anything. You are where you are, right now, for a reason. God arranged you there. And wherever you are, whether it be on a mountaintop or in a valley, you can offer something. So think about it and pray about it: what can you offer today?

A-C-T-I-O-N

Now, there's just one final point I really want to hit home, and it may be the sum of everything I've written so far: to start the road to recovery, you need to take that first step. You need to take *action*.

Action is a loaded word and may even lead to some anxiety right off the bat. For starters, imagine your image of "action." Take that image, pretend it's a glass, and smash it with a baseball bat. Action doesn't necessarily mean radical. So take a deep breath. I want action to look like something new. I want it to be simple.

Depending on where you are with your mental illness, your first step of action may just be admitting you have a problem. You may have to admit your anxiety/depression/OCD/PTSD/addiction is out of control. You may have to face your illness in a whole new light and ask for help, and that's okay! There's no shame in struggling with something. All struggles mean is that you're still alive and breathing and that God isn't done with you.

Action may mean calling a friend or family member and asking for additional help. Maybe you need their help with some financial issues while you find time to take care of yourself. Maybe you can call your parents and they can watch the kids for a couple days while you rest. Maybe you can call someone in your small group to come over and pray with you. Again, action can be as simple as praying.

Don't let me fool you, though, because I'm still sick. My anxiety and depression are not 100 percent under control. Just this past week, I had several bouts of deep anxiety that led to hard questions about my path and my future, but I'm still fighting and I'm not going to give up. I'm still going to my support groups. I'm still seeing my counselor and shrink. I'm still doing breathing exercises. I still pray and ask for prayer and spend time with God *every* day. All of those are steps of action and steps to healing.

Healing is a journey, but don't see it as a destination. Each day can be a victory. And it's okay if each day's not. There will be bad days, but there will also be good days. Take it all just one day at a time.

A Voice from the Valley

All I know is doing nothing is not the answer. If you sit with your illness and live in denial or pity, it's going to come and bite you good. It happened to me. Years and years I stuffed my feelings until they got the best of me and brought me to the emergency room. It's incredibly important to take action, because no one can take it for you. It's up to you.

No one can force you to get healthy. If you want to live in constant fear and depression and anger and pain, that's on you. But if you want to try and break free, you need to do something, and maybe that something is just a little prayer to break the ice. Maybe it's a little prayer that says, "God, I'm lost and I'm hurting. Please guide me to healing." There you go. There's your foothold. Now push off from there and go.

In Matthew 9, Jesus heals a man born blind. Jesus spat on the ground, made mud, and rubbed it on the man's eyes. Then Jesus told the man to go wash in a specific place. Verse 7 says, "So the man went and washed and came home seeing." What if the man would have ignored Jesus? Would he have been able to see? Jesus made the man take action—he made the man show his faith. The man did: he washed and then could see.

What action can you take today? Can you join a support group? Can you make an appointment to see somebody? Can you ask for help? Can you simply pray to our loving God?

If there's no action, there's no healing. Take a step and show your faith. Just a small step to start. And be proud of that. The greatest journeys ever taken all began with a single step.

They're Dimming the Lights Now

All right, that's it. Show's over. Be sure to tip your servers. Didn't they do a wonderful job?

I've been thinking about this conclusion for a few days. What do I want the lasting taste to be? And, in his own way, God provided the answer.

I was sitting in church yesterday, not exactly zeroed in on the sermon, so I started flipping through my Bible. I was thinking about this finale. I was looking for a verse or passage, but I didn't know what it was going to be until I found it, and once I did, I knew it—I *absolutely* knew it. It's a bit lengthy, but please take the time to read it all:

> Be merciful to me, O Lord, for I am in distress; my eyes grow weak with sorrow, my soul and my body with grief. My life is consumed by anguish and my years by groaning; my strength fails because of my affliction, and my bones grow weak. Because of all my enemies, I am the utter contempt of my neighbors; I am a dread to my friends—those who see me on the street flee from me. I am forgotten by them as though I were dead; I have become like broken pottery. For I hear the slander of many; there is terror on every side; they conspire against me and plot to take my life. But I trust in you, O Lord; I say, 'You are my God.' My times are in your hands. (Psalm 31:9–15a)

What strength and faith David has in his God. David is in utter distress and chaos, he's at his weakest point in life—his most vulnerable point—and yet, after all is said and done, he writes, "But I trust in you, O Lord."

Just because I'm writing this doesn't mean I'm "over" my anxiety, or that I've beaten it. I'm not a hundred percent healed, and I *never* will be, not on this earth, but I want whatever comes against me to know that, no matter what, I'm going to trust in my God first.

Anxiety's still there, knocking at the door, but I'm going to trust in my God. Depression is creeping up again, but I'm going to trust in my God. PTSD's keeping me up nights, but I'm going to trust in my God. This addiction is gnawing on me like a dog on its bone, but I'm going to trust in my God. The devil is telling me to give up and that I can't do it, but I'm going to trust in my God.

David ends his Psalm with, "Be strong and take heart, all you who hope in the Lord" (verse 24). You can't hope in people, medications, or yourself. The only way you can begin to recover is by

A Voice from the Valley

letting God take the wheel, by hoping and trusting in him. He's got this. Let him take it.

Surrender. Every day (a hundred times a day if you have to), surrender. Give it up to God. Humble yourself enough to say, "You know what? I can't do it on my own anymore. I *need* God to handle this." And that's not weakness saying that—that's the strongest faith there is saying that.

Some days will be better than others, but know you're not alone. I'm here in the valley with you, lifting up my voice and saying, "Praise God. I'm surrendering it to him." And because of that, I will fear no evil. My God is greater and my God is stronger than anything that has risen, or will rise, against me. He is the king of all, and he loves me for me, and I *know* I'm safe with him.

Praying for you, always.

—Tim Dustin

Afterword

FOUR-AND-A-HALF YEARS LATER. I can't believe it. It's been four-and-a-half years since I put down those last words:

> *Praying for you, always.*
> —Tim Dustin

So, where am I now? Well, I'm furloughed. Collecting unemployment. Trying to keep the house up while my wife works. Waiting for a President to be announced while they count ballots. Wondering who to see, and who not to see, during this pandemic.

But through all that, God hasn't stopped. It's been during these past months of being furloughed that I got in touch with my counselor, and he gave me a couple places to submit my book to, *A Voice from the Valley*. And now, here it is, in print, in your hands.

Where am I now? Yeah, things are tough (they're tough everywhere), but I have never been more spiritually and mentally healthy in my entire life.

Life is hard, and we honestly have no idea what's around the next corner, but I trust in God, and he's seen that next corner before I ever even got in the car.

It may be four-and-a-half years later, in a seemingly completely different world, but the message remains the same: surrender to God and trust in him, and his love, one day at a time.

By doing that, I've bought a house. I've gotten married. I've adopted a dog. I've gotten a full time job. I've traveled to places I never thought I could. I've been living an adult life which always seemed so far away and out of reach. And how? Through grace, and being imperfect, and placing it all at God's feet.

Afterword

I still keep in touch with my counselor, I'm still on medication, I still have to slow down and not get ahead of myself, but I'm at a place now I never thought possible. The world is in panic all around, but I feel a peace that can only come from God.

I know God has me. He had me four-and-a-half years ago, during the lowest points of my life, and you know what? He has me now, too. He's not going to let me go. No.

Since originally finishing this book, I've spoken and given my testimony at various support and recovery groups. I've shared my story with my work staff. I've had deep and meaningful conversations about faith and hope with complete strangers, some of them being non-Christians. Because I offered myself to God, and continue to do so, he's taken my mess and turned it into an incredible story of hope and love through him.

I'm not over anxiety or depression, or feel like I'm standing on the top, but I know, in the end, it's going to be okay. And why? Because Jesus loves me, this I know. Wherever I go, he's right there. He's got me. He's still on the throne.

I'm writing this *afterward* to encourage. I was at my lowest point those years ago, a step away from utter darkness, but, through God, here I am, writing this, four-and-a-half years later. It wasn't easy, and it didn't happen overnight. There were setbacks—there are still setbacks. There were more struggles and tears and battles, and those will be in my future, too, but wherever you are, you *can* do it! Through God, all things are possible. That means if you're somewhere in the valley, you can rise higher, you can push on, you can accomplish things you never thought possible, and I know that *because I was there*! I never thought I'd hold a steady job, or get married, or buy a house. None of that. But I did it.

Each day, I said, "God, I can't do this alone. You know that. Please, strengthen me, for today." And he did. And he does, each and every day.

At the beginning of this work, I quoted my grandfather, who said, "Before I was ever born, God had his eye on this sparrow." And that's where I want to end this work, too.

Afterword

I don't know what's coming next, but God is still watching me, he still sees me, he still hears me, and he still loves me. I may fall, I may relapse in thinking, but his mercy will be there. I may panic, but his guidance will be there. I may try and do things my own way, but his love will be there.

Know he loves you. Know perfect peace can be found in him. Know rest can be found in him.

So take heart, child, our God is sovereign, and he's still on the throne.

Acknowledgements

THIS BOOK EXISTS BECAUSE of my Lord and savior, Jesus Christ. For me, my recovery is dependent on him and my relationship with him. God, *thanks* is not a big enough word for what you've done for me. May this book be an offering you find acceptable.

I'd like to thank my counselor, Matt, for his nudging me to write "my story," and then to publish "my story." I don't think this work would exist without you.

I'd like to thank my past counselor, Chris, as well as my shrink-wrap, Tom—both of you played a crucial role in getting me to a place of sanity.

I'd like to thank my parents for their leadership and continued grace. I also need to thank the rest of my family and my extended family—you've all played a role in this book and in my life, in one way or another.

I need to highlight my friend Leah. You've been an encouragement to me and our friendship is a true blessing.

To Natalie, thank you so much for your strength and peace when I was/am weak. You were there during my toughest moments and decided to marry me anyway. I know there is no challenge we can't overcome together, through Christ.

My Tuesday recovery group (you know who you are), I'm eternally grateful. Just being heard has meant so much. I pray nothing but peace and continued healing for all of you.

I need to thank Wipf & Stock. Where other publishers passed on this book, you all saw it as an opportunity to help and encourage others. Thank you.

Acknowledgements

Mort Castle, you are a truly inspiring and dedicated writer and teacher. I'm so grateful to know you.

I want to thank my past writing professors: Kyle Beachy, Christian TeBordo, Gary Johnson, and the marvelous others. I would not be the writer I am today without all of you. Thank you.

I feel credit is absolutely due to Louie Giglio, T.D. Jakes, Vincent P. Collins, and Rick Warren. Your works have been true inspirations.

Others writers that have inspired me are Oscar Wilde, Ernest Hemingway, J. M. Barrie, J.D. Salinger, Daniel Keyes, and Marilynne Robinson. Your works are honest and true.

I need to also thank Chris Tomlin, Matt Maher, David Crowder, Bellarive, Blue Tree, Audio Adrenaline, Switchfoot, Hillsong, Newsboys, Michael W. Smith, Rhett Walker Band, Steven Curtis Chapman, The Digital Age, John Mark McMillan, Jesus Culture, Haste the Day, Corpus Christi, Close Your Eyes, Sleeping Giant, The Chariot, Rocky Votolato, Pink Floyd, B.B. King, and the Man in Black himself, Johnny Cash. All of you, your music inspires and I am grateful.

There are other musicians and writers and individuals and this list could go on and on for pages. I'm just so grateful to everyone that's somehow played a role in my life, for better or for worse—I'm the man I am today because of all of you. And you know what? I wouldn't change any of it. If this book helps one person (as cliché as it sounds), everything was worth it.

You, the reader. Yeah, *you*. I'm thankful to you, too. And know I'm praying for you. In addition, I want to hear *your* story. Reach out and let me know where you're at with your struggle, and how this book has helped/is helping. You can write me at: timdustinwrites@gmail.com

Remember, we're all in this valley together. Let's just take it a breath and a step at a time. Sound good?

"You will keep in *perfect peace* him whose mind is steadfast, because he trusts in you" (Isaiah 26:3).

May God truly bless you all.

www.ingramcontent.com/pod-product-compliance
Lightning Source LLC
Chambersburg PA
CBHW072036060426
42449CB00010BA/2299